Six Secrets
Of G.E.N.I.U.S.

Many of the stories and concepts
provided in this book are found in the
award-winning bestseller

Awaken the Genius
By Patrick K. Porter, Ph.D

Illustrations by Dean Sylvia

Published by:
Positive Changes Hypnosis®
3150 Laurel Road
Shipman, VA 22971
800-771-7866
www.postitivechanges.com
&
Anglo-American Books
Underwood, St. Clears
Carmathen, Dyfed
UK SA334NE
www.anglo-american.co.uk

For more information on where Dr. Porter will be
leading workshops in your area call 800-771-7866
(USA) and become a part of the awakening of the
planet...you could be the person who changes the
world's thinking forever!

ISBN: 1-888316-00-4
Printed in the United States of America
10 9 8 7 6 5 4 3

TABLE OF CONTENTS

"Men are often capable of greater things than they perform. They are sent into the world with bills of credit, and seldom draw to their full extent."

HORACE WALPOLE

WELCOME TO
THE SIX SECRETS
OF GENIUS!

Genius is a higher order of thinking. Beyond survival and success there is a synergy that we all draw upon. This work didn't start with me and most certainly won't end with this text. Surely Einstein and Tesla and the other great adventurers didn't invent it either--it is an inherent part of human nature.

I am grateful to have been born into such a phenomenal time known as the "information explosion," and to share in the techniques that helped me awaken my learning potential. I am grateful for the inspiration and wisdom of many thinkers and trainers who have shaped my life.

--Patrick Porter

"We know what we are,
but know not what we may be. "

William Shakespeare

INITIATION

There once was an old fix-it man known to everyone in the town as "Old Joe." Joe could fix anything, but he was especially good with pipes. It was the middle of winter and the boiler in the grade school building would not work. They tried everything, but all of their attempts failed. Finally, in desperation, they called Old Joe. After they told him of all their efforts, Joe scratched his head a few times and walked up and down the length of the boiler. He walked back to his toolbox, took out his hammer and walked back down the length of the machine. Then, without any warning, he took his hammer and tapped gently on a valve. Instantly, the boiler started back up and continued to run without hesitation. Joe packed up his tools and went home.

A week went by and the school received the bill from Old Joe. It was for $1,000.00. They were furious to say the least. The matter was referred to the superintendent who telephoned Joe and asked for an itemized statement. How could the cost possibly have been $1,000.00 when all he did was tap his hammer once? Old Joe agreed, and being the simple man that he was, sent a simple statement. He charged $1.00 for the hammer tap and $999.00 for knowing where to tap!

WHAT IS THE RIGHT TOOL?

The story of Old Joe is the perfect example of the G.E.N.I.U.S. mind-set. What is most important is to know where to intervene and then to use the right tools. Many people have tried to create changes in their life by changing jobs, relationships, cars--you name it they have changed it. It's great to know when you need a change, but it is a totally different story to know what to change.

I believe the what to change is your MIND, and the best tool to enhance the working of your mind is your thoughts. Your thoughts are tools your mind uses to create the way in which you interact with reality. Your thoughts, just like all tools, can be used to build or to destroy. You are the judge. Geniuses recognize their thoughts as a powerful force for change and use them to create the future they desire.

These secrets of genius are dedicated to people who are ready to acknowledge that life involves a series of problems and are willing to create solutions.

THE WILD STALLION

Imagine you are strapped in a saddle atop a wild stallion. You are grasping the reigns, your feet are tight in the stirrups, and your knees are clinging to the animal's sides. Sweat pours from your brow as you concentrate on keeping yourself balanced in the saddle. The more you try to make that wild bronco bend to your will, the more difficult it becomes.

Your mind can be just like that wild pony. It will do what it has rehearsed (or always done)--which is not always what you intend! Too, if you are spending all of your energy just trying to control the beast, how much benefit can you get from it?

One sharp fellow refers to this phenomena as the "Monkey Mind." We all experience it from time to time. The mind jumps hither and tither. Our focus is fleeting. One thought leads to another and then another. Soon we've forgotten our original goal. Perhaps this is why scientists say we use less than 10% of our mind's potential.

How does one tame the wild monkeys of the mind? How do we tap that untamed 90% of mind power? The first step is to start a program of thinking differently. Develop what we call possibility thinking.

Here's your chance to get started. Read through the following story slowly. Test your patience. Allow your mind time to absorb the flavor and sensation of each word. Give yourself time to ponder each thought. It will be your first step in training that wild pony.

Long ago there were two boys who were the best of friends. One boy was born with the destiny of becoming a great emperor like his father. The other was the son of a lame juggler whose injuries were caused years earlier while saving his emperor's life. The emperor had looked upon the juggler with overwhelming gratitude and visited him every day during his painful recovery. One day he knelt at the injured man's side. Touching his royal palm to the juggler's head, he vowed to care for him and his family for as long as it was within his power.

Thus the juggler's son came to live in the resplendent palace and to make friends with the emperor's son.

The boys were inseparable. Every day was a new adventure and the emperor and his court usually overlooked the boys' mischief. The lame juggler had taught his son the arts of juggling, acrobatics, dance and comedy. The boy was a natural. He spent hours performing his tricks for the emperor's son who would giggle, applaud and stomp his feet. At times he laughed until he had to pant for breath. Then yet another antic would send him into peels of laughter all over again. On one such occasion the future emperor suddenly stopped smiling, took the jester by the arm and gazed directly into his eyes. "Whatever may come," he said, "vow that we shall always be friends...No! Better yet, family . . . brothers!"

As his father had done before him, he made a solemn oath. "I will always protect you and care for you like my own family...of this I vow." He then laid his palm upon his friend's brow, at the same time taking the boy's hand and placing it upon his own forehead. "Do you vow the same?"

"Yes," he murmured. "I vow." For what else could he say to his imperial friend.

As the boys grew into men they remained true to their vow. The two men married on the same day, at the same time. One behind fortress walls and the other in the village square with music and merriment that echoed through the streets until dawn. One year later they were each granted the joyous gift of a strong, healthy son.

The villagers mourned the passing of the old emperor for he was a kind and just ruler. Yet they quickly came to trust their young, new emperor as he carried on his father's legacy. The bond between the two friends grew ever stronger. The man who was now a renowned juggler and acrobat would often perform for his emperor and the noble applause always brought him the greatest joy.

For many years it was peaceful and prosperous throughout the land. Rumors about a rebellious uprising reached the emperor from time to time but the varied reports of contentedness among his people quickly mollified his concern.

Both sons grew into strong and capable men and they too were to be the closest of friends. The juggler's son chose the life of a warrior. While his imperial friend was groomed to one day rule the land, he spent his days learning the warrior's art. His aim was to be a mighty protector for the regal family he had grown to love.

One day a storm of angry men swarmed about the palace. "Freedom!" was their cry. "We demand an end to tyranny!"

A great battle ensued with the juggler's son leading the emperor's soldiers. Desperately they fought against the insurrection. Swords clashed, screams resounded, and hundreds of powerful men fell to the ground, crumpled and groaning. The leader fought with anguish and rage. Then, in an instant, his head snapped up and he stared in horror at a bearded dissenter, his arm wrapped around the throat of an elegant young man as he dragged him to the balcony edge. "Look, I've got the emperor's son!"

The juggler's son swiftly put an end to his battle with the rebel before him. He dashed up the staircase, taking three and four steps at a time. He was too late. Just as his hand grabbed at the filthy collar, the rebel hoisted his captive's feet over the edge and shoved. The juggler's son had just a moment's glimpse into the anguished eyes of his friend, and then he was gone.

The rebellion lasted but one day, but the mourning went on for months. The emperor's grief overwhelmed him, not only for the loss of his son, but for what the law of the land decreed that he must do. He anguished over the pain he would cause his blood brother. This was what he could barely withstand. He called the men that represented three generations to the palace; an aged, disfigured juggler, the emperor's closest friend and the condemned.

He gazed at the younger man squarely. "As leader of my army, you were directly responsible for protecting the future emperor. You have failed. For this reason, I must sentence you to death."

"No!" cried the crippled old man. "Your father once vowed to protect my family. Please, carry out his promise and let my grandson live!"

"This I cannot do," said the emperor, gazing sadly into the old man's eyes. "It is out of my hands."

"However, in honor of the vow my father made to you, and the promise that I once made to your son, I will grant you both the choice of method for his death. By mid-day tomorrow you will declare the means by which your progeny shall die."

A tear streamed down his cheek as he gazed upon his blood brother. He knew his offer meant little consolation. "Go now, and return tomorrow to these same chambers with your decision."

"No," said the condemned one's father. He lifted his chin, cleared his throat and, gazing directly into the eyes of his life-long friend, declared, "I have already made my choice."

"Please, think upon your decision..." The emperor pleaded.

"Yes," said the crippled one, his voice catching for a moment. "Why be so hasty in our decision? We must contemplate the way in which our beloved shall have the least pain!"

The younger juggler was adamant and so finally the emperor agreed to allow the death decree to be made.

"I wish," he said, "that my son shall die of old age."

And so it was done.

***

As you read through the story did you use the same possibility thinking as the juggler? Or did the wild stallion race ahead, planning the method for a quick and painless demise? If you found the ending to the story gave you a shift in your perception, then you have experienced a reframe. Which, by the way, means that you have already started a program for possibility thinking! A reframe is a term used to describe a situation about which your conscious mind has preconceived notions and that, with the shifting of meaning or words, places you into another frame of reference.

The reason a joke makes you laugh is because they pulled a reframe on you. You thought the joke was going in one direction, and then it suddenly came at you from another.

Question: What has 18 legs and catches flies? (You're thinking of an insect, right?)

Answer: A baseball team! (Reframe)

The juggler and Old Joe have a few things in common. They both know how to use tools. Old Joe used the hammer to tap just the right place, the young juggler used the tools of *language* and *reframing*.

Are you ready to reframe your life? What if someone told you this about your past:

In the past you *always* did the very best you could. You *always* made the best decisions possible.

Do you believe it? Most people will say, no way! I could have done this or that differently. Let's look at your past from a new perspective.

What if you reframed your memories? We all know hindsight is 20/20. But what if you were back in the experience right now. You're where there is no hindsight, right? What if you consider only the information available to you at the time?

When you look at your life in this way, all your past memories are reframed! Feelings of guilt instantly vanish. Your self-esteem grows by leaps and bounds because yes, you always did your very best!"

By reading this book you are learning to use an unlimited genius place. I call it your personal "cyber-space." It exists between your ears. It is the *other-than-conscious* mind. It is the magical realm called *imagination.* Reframing takes place here. Your *genuine positive attitude* is reawakened here. In "cyber-space" you enter the realm of *infinite possibility.* Imagine, in any one moment in time there is only an infinite number of possibilities!

Enter your personal "cyber-space," spark your imagination, and awaken to the infinite possibility that you are a genuine genius!

These secrets are for those who are ready to develop a 21st Century mind-set; those who want to step out of the prison of their conscious mind and into the realm of "cyber-space." This is the world of the imagination, where creativity and inventiveness abound. Are you ready to awaken the other level of your mind--the level that exists outside of time and knows no restrictions or limitations?

"True genius sees with the eyes of a child and thinks with the brain of a genii."

Puzant Kevork Thomajan

SECRET #1
ACTIVATING YOUR GENIUS

G -- STANDS FOR GENUINE POSITIVE ATTITUDE

Once upon a time when the world was young there lived a brave and mighty ruler. King Optima reigned over the Realm of Possibility. The King ruled with wisdom and patience. Consequently the Realm of Possibility held unlimited freedom of choice. At times even the King was overwhelmed by the variety of options available to him.

King Optima had gained wisdom beyond his years. To be a fair king, he knew he would require an advisor. He imagined a gifted seer who was wise and free from prejudice. But where would he find one with such talents?

Word spread throughout the land. The King was seeking the wisest man or woman in the land to become his counselor. The seer would need special gifts. He or she must see the past, present and future in order to guide the King in all ways.

There was no better place to live than the Realm of Possibility. Wise men and women traveled from the farthest reaches of the earth. Each prayed for a chance appointment with the King. One after the other stood before Optima boasting of this skill or that talent. The King grew weary. Perhaps a true wise seer did not exist.

Then a youth with shining eyes and a bright smile appeared.

The King's voice boomed in frustration. "How, pray tell, would a boy such as you be qualified to advise the mighty King Optima? What are your qualifications?

"I have but one qualification," answered the boy softly. "I stand firm in the truth. I never lie."

The King stroked his beard thoughtfully. "How might this serve the Realm of Possibility?"

The bright lad replied, "Whatever happens, whatever the concern, I will simply remind you, all for a good purpose."

The King mulled this over. What a great conscience, he thought. The lad will be at my side through every decision and circumstance reminding me that everything that happens is for a good purpose. With this I will surely remain positive. Thus I will be a fair and just king for the Realm of Possibility.

"Yes," his voice thundered, "You may have the position of counselor." He hesitated a moment. "First, however, you must agree to swear an oath that you will stay true. No matter the circumstance, whatever the occasion, whether you believe it to be good or bad, you will always remind me, "All for a good purpose."

"Absolutely!" The boy bowed to his master. "I shall be true."

As the years passed the King and his counselor became close friends. The advisor's statement, all for a good purpose, served King Optima well. After months of insurrection, the King was faced with the decision to protect his people by declaring war. It was a time of great turmoil. The decision weighed heavily on his heart. He looked to his counselor for advice.

With a soft smile and kind eyes the seer replied simply, "All for a good purpose, sire. All for a good purpose."

Optima immediately felt relief from his heavy decision. He could not know whether declaring this war would have a positive or negative outcome. Yet his counselor reminded him that all was for a good purpose.

The war was brutal but brief. The Realm of Possibility had triumphed. The Kingdom was serene once again.

One evening the King was eating dinner with his counselor at his side. While cutting a large loaf of crusty bread the knife slipped and sliced Optima's thumb clear through. The King stared at his severed thumb in disbelief. His anger and grief were overwhelming. The pain and shock burned through his body. He turned to his counselor.

"All for a good purpose, sire," spoke the seer calmly.

"What?" Optima shouted. "How dare you declare this for a good purpose!" He thrust his bleeding hand at the counselor.

His shout startled his court into action. One of the royal servants wrapped a stiff white napkin around the profusely bleeding hand. "Hurry," she called, "get the surgeon!"

Optima's rage shook him. With his free hand he grabbed the counselor by the collar. "Off to the dungeon with him. I do not wish to see his face ever again!" He shoved the mute seer toward his guards. "Make sure he gets nothing but bread and water." The guards surrounded the youth and guided him through the doorway. The king's voice roared after them, "We'll see what's for a good purpose!"

Months passed and the King slowly adapted to using his fingers minus the thumb. Optima's hand healed, but his heart did not. The counselor had so thoroughly enraged him he could not find forgiveness in his heart. He would not admit how much he missed his trusted companion.

The young counselor remained in the dank dungeon with only crusts of moldy bread to eat. His hair and beard grew long and grizzly. His once immaculate garments were coated in grime. All was quiet in the tiny cell.

Tuesday was King Optima's hunting day. As was his habit, he mounted his stead and headed for the Realm's forest. The forest was unusually quiet on this particular Tuesday. He marveled at the silence. Where was the usual scuttle of grouse and ground squirrel?

From the silence there came forth a wild, hysterical scream. In an instant aborigine headhunters surrounded King Optima. Each held a straight spear with a glinting arrowhead. Optima's mighty white horse reared up only once. It seemed even he felt the defeat in that moment.

One aborigine was covered with paint. Scores of small clay beads circled his neck. He leaned on his spear with an arrogance that was clearly absent from the others. It was obvious to Optima that this was the leader. He heard him grunt a command. The warriors reached up and yanked Optima from the saddle.

The leader pointed his spear at Optima. He moved closer. His black eyes examined the royal clothing and the crown that adorned his head. He turned to the others and began his manic screaming once again.

At first the King thought he had angered the leader. When the warriors began cheering he realized it was much worse. They knew they had captured someone of great power and wealth. The horror of it washed over King Optima. To a headhunter, he was the perfect specimen.

Optima stumbled as the headhunters pushed him onward. By the time they reached the encampment he was exhausted. His throat was parched.

The headhunters began chanting an eerie cry. King Optima knew the end was at hand. The entire village was present for the event. Two young warriors stood on each side of him. They turned him so that he faced an immense chopping block. The leader stood with an enormous ax at his shoulder.

Optima laid his head upon the block and closed his eyes. The leader's eyes were ablaze as he hoisted the heavy ax over his head. Just as he began to thrust the ax forward, the warrior beside Optima let out a screech.

Optima's eyes popped open. The young warrior was frantically pointing at Optima's hand.

The leader stormed over to the warrior. His coal eyes shone with anger. He listened to the young headhunter intently and then turned his attention to Optima's scarred hand. The leader howled and shoved Optima off the block.

The warriors took the cue from their leader. They took turns pushing and shoving him. He stumbled and hit the ground with a thud. Confusion muddled his brain. It was as if they were throwing him out of the encampment.

Finally Optima realized that without his thumb he was not the perfect specimen! That was why they were so angry. In one move he jumped up and began running toward the forest. He didn't know if anyone followed. He just ran.

When Optima finally stopped running their angry screams were distant. He was safe. They had not followed.

Optima practically skipped his way back to his palace. Just as the sun was setting he heard someone call his name.

"Over here! I'm over here," he called back.

Optima ran to the dungeon. He flung the barred gate open. The counselor was so weak he could barely raise his head.

"Wise Counselor," Optima cried. "You were right! It was all for a good purpose!" The guilt and shame coursed through him as he told the seer the story of the vicious headhunters and his unexpected release.

"Please," he begged, "Please forgive me! You can't imagine how sorry I am . . ." Optima's voice trailed off.

The wise one sat serenely. A broad smile played boldly on his lips.

"Why are you smiling?" Optima scratched his head in confusion. "How can you sit there and smile after all I have put you through? What about the pain and discomfort you have endured?" Tears welled in Optima's eyes. "You are so weak. You cannot even stand. You are covered in grime. From where does this smile come, after the kind of suffering you have withstood?"

"Why sire," the counselor laughed. "Had I not been here in this dungeon I would have been out hunting with you on Tuesday." He looked at Optima squarely. "I would have been the perfect specimen!"

* * *

Very few people ever reach the status of "genius." There are many factors that prevent people from using their full genius potential. I believe the main deterrent is fear. Fear comes in many shapes, forms and sizes. Fear infiltrates, paralyzes and destroys; it oozes into the deepest core of the human potential, freezes all creativity, and then expands out into every thought and action. What follows next is the destructive side effect of fear. It is indecision.

When the main ingredients to life are *personal growth* and *wisdom* the status of "genius" will be earned. Growth and achievement make life a true adventure. A *genuine positive attitude* is the natural side effect. Wouldn't it be easier to make decisions from this frame of reference?

Geniuses know that now is the best starting point for a bright and exciting future. I invite you to awaken your genius potential. It's there within you. I know it is. We are all imbued with the ability to shine. Start by shaking your old beliefs loose. Focus on the kind of genius that exists within you. Realize that your genius is unique and genuinely different from anyone else's genius.

How would your life improve if you went about assuming that everything you experience is for a good purpose? You may not know the purpose right now. Do you really need to know?

If you find it hard to believe that you could possibly be a genius, think again. When I was in the second grade, I was held back. My parents were told that I had a learning disability. I considered myself a "victim" of the system. I was the class clown.

What I have since done with my life is nothing short of a miracle, Secret #1 is what created the person I am today. Without it I could not have earned two doctorate degrees. I would never have written this book. It would have been impossible for me to fulfill my life-long dream of a career helping people. I didn't awaken my genius over night, but it did happen and is still happening.

The truth is, we are all moving; some people are going forward, some backward, and some wherever the advertisers tell them to go. Are you ready to realize the limitlessness of your potential? The only "limits" are those you choose through your own thoughts, actions and beliefs. A genius knows life is a game. There are no winners or losers, no victims or martyrs; life gives in the exact proportion that we ask. Geniuses are simply people who have learned to ask the right questions -- of the world and of themselves. Time is their ally.

Understand that you were born with the knowledge of Secret #1. Think of how much you have learned since the moment you were born! You had to start by learning to use all the different muscles of your body. It's hard to imagine, but at one time you had to learn to stand up. It took courage to pull yourself upright, but you finally did it.

Once you were up, your legs may have felt weak. Maybe you weren't even sure that you could stand like the other people around you. But, because everyone else could stand, you continued to think and act as if you could too. You grew stronger and steadier. Once you met the challenge of standing, you began to notice how other people could move about on their feet. You tried it once and fell down. Perhaps you cried. That didn't stop you. You tried again, and again. Still you fell down.

In one incredible moment, you mastered the art of balance and took off across the floor. In that instant, something magical happened. Your brain stored the success of walking and junked out all past failures.

So a genuine positive attitude is natural to you! You used it when you learned to talk, to eat by yourself, to ride a bike and to tie your shoelaces. And you remembered to forget all your failures. Now that you have reawakened your genuine positive attitude, you will remember that there is no such thing as failure, there is only feedback.

My father once told me that a person who works from the neck down can expect to earn up to $20 per hour, while the person who works from the neck up can earn without limit. This made a lot of sense to me. Especially after seeing my father come home from the factory day after day complaining that he wasn't making enough money. At that time he was truly stuck. He was actively living out what he perceived his life to be. He spent half his life at the factory with people just as stuck as he was, and the other half in a bottle. He remained that way, trapped in a life of his own making, until years later when he was willing to trust in his genius. He stopped drinking with the twelve-step program of Alcoholics Anonymous, went back to college, and then started a business helping people to help themselves.

When you trust in your mind it will be true to you, and that is when you will rediscover your genuine positive attitude. The assumption that all is for a good purpose will naturally follow.

Every genius had to take the first step. You can start with realizing that you are far more capable than you have been led to believe.

Become willing to stretch the limits to the max in order to achieve your goals.

"When I was young I observed that nine out of every ten things I did were failures, so I did ten times more work."

GEORGE BERNARD SHAW

SECRET #2
FOCUS YOUR GENIUS

E -- STANDS FOR ENTHUSIASM, FOCUS & FLEXIBILITY

Sammy Sly has a goal. He is certain that one day he will achieve it. He knows he has set his sights high and the neighbors often ridicule him for trying, but still he is determined. One day he will see the Statue of Liberty. So every morning the buzz of his alarm awakens him at sunrise. He tidies his little two-room apartment, then showers, shaves, and eats a healthy breakfast. With upturned chin and light feet, he steps out into the bright sunshine, savoring the warmth and ignoring the smog of the day. He sets a straight course for the bus stop. Forty-seven minutes later he steps down onto sand-covered pavement and draws a deep breath of the salty ocean spray. Sammy spends his day combing the shoreline, ever hopeful that today he will discover the majestic statue of his dreams.

At mid-afternoon, Sammy's confidence becomes overshadowed by a familiar sense of gloom. He stops, stretches and gazes down the expanse of open beach. Off in the distance he can see the Santa Monica Pier. With an ache in his chest he turns to look upon the expanse of city behind him. He can just glimpse the highest peaks of the Hollywood Hills. At sunset Sammy boards the bus for home. He climbs the steps with leaden feet. His shoulders droop as he slumps into his seat. Hot tears of frustration stream down his flushed cheeks. Upon arriving home Sammy's landlady, Mrs. White, waves to him and quickly turns back to her gardening. Long ago she had given up on trying to convince Sammy that perhaps he should move his search elsewhere.

Will Sammy ever find the Statue of Liberty? Of course not. He is determined, steadfast, and absolutely certain that his goal will be achieved. He starts his day with an abundance of enthusiasm. Yet he is 3,000 miles off course. Sammy forgot to focus his enthusiasm in the direction of his goal. He was not flexible enough to investigate Mrs. White's ideas.

Did you know that technicians who program missiles are always assuming that the missile is off its course? They check and re-check the course and coordinates. They calmly make course corrections when necessary. Because of this assumption, the missiles almost always reach their target. What do you think might happen if you began to "program" your life in this way--on the assumption that you just might be off course? You would probably end up making continuous assessments of yourself, your goals and actions, so that you too can reach your target. You would be enthusiastic, focused and flexible.

If a genius wants to see a sunrise, he doesn't jump out of bed in the morning and start running in just any direction. He may end up running west and missing the sunrise completely.

A genius awakens with the belief that everything he needs is available to him. If he needs a course correction, it's a snap. If he is lacking some skill or ability he doesn't cry, "Why Me?" He takes inventory of himself and asks, "Why not me?" He then sets out on a new course that will provide any help, guidance or training he might need. Consider what Thomas Edison once said, "Genius is 1% inspiration and 99% perspiration!"

If you had a bank that credited your account each morning with $86,400, that carried over no balance from day to day, allowed you to keep no cash in your account, and every evening canceled whatever part of the amount you failed to use during the day, what would you do? Draw out every cent, of course! Well, you have such a bank, and its name is "Time." Every morning it credits you with 86,400 seconds. Every night it rules off as lost whatever you have failed to invest to good purpose. It carries over no balance. It allows no overdraft. Each day it opens a new account with you. Each night it bums the records of the day. If you fail to use the day's deposits the loss is yours. There is no going back. There is no drawing against "tomorrow." You must live in the present, on today's deposit.

You have made an investment in yourself and your family by purchasing this book. It is more than the price paid; it is an investment in your time, which is one commodity you cannot buy. Time is given to you free of charge, and what you do with it is up to you.

"Those who want to secure pearls from the sea have to dive deep to fetch them. It does not help them to dabble among the shallow waves near the shore and say that the sea has no pearls and all stories about them are false."

-- Sai Baba

What is meant by this simple example? That there will always be those people who believe in the struggle of life and little else. They will tell you, "That's impossible," and "You can't do that!" or, "Accept it, kid, that's just the way life is. You can't change it!" To these people, there is only one way to live--their way. These are the people who are not willing to dive deep to fetch their pearls.

I am here to tell you that the finest, shiniest pearls are the ones you must dive into the deepest depths to find. They are there, just waiting for you to fetch them. The secret is in putting it all together to work for you. This is how you create a state of *infinite abundance*. This simple statement, *infinite abundance*, means that there is plenty--for you and for me, and plenty of everything. Unfortunately, infinite abundance is not the present belief of our society.

We all possess the ability to attract into our lives what we need. However, this is not always what we want. This is how people get themselves into trouble. It is how we lose *focus*. Probably the greatest tool the genius possesses is the understanding that we are always in the right place at the right time, and will always have what we need. This may be a difficult concept for those people who have always held true to their philosophy that someone or something else controls them.

Some people believe that their parents, spouse, friends, teachers, the government or other authorities are in control of their lives. They have a whole arsenal of excuses and are loaded and ready to blame another person for their shortcomings. They will tell you that their mother didn't love them or that their father was never home, that none of their teachers ever cared about them and most people, they are certain, were out to get them.

Still others allow circumstance to control their lives. These are the "if only," people. *I would have ...if only my parents had not divorced when I was ten. I could have ...if only it had not rained that day. I would try ...if only I had better luck. I could get a better job . . .if only I lived in a different city. I'm sure my life would work ...if only I could win the lottery!*

The habits of self-imposed limitation and of blaming others are probably the main reasons why there are so few people in the world recognized as "Genius." The reality, however, is that every one of us is encoded with the genius potential. This capacity is natural and readily available within us at our summoning. It is very real and even tangible once one becomes aware of its presence. This potential can be likened to a seed. Within one seed from an oak tree is the potential for millions of mighty trees. Yet, if it is not germinated, it can't possibly sprout, grow roots, build a trunk and branches, form leaves, or create the seeds for its future generations. I find that as I regularly dive for pearls and nurture the seeds I have planted, the opportunities I need are always there; often before I know that I need them!

While I was writing *Awaken the Genius*, I experienced one of those magical moments when everything seems to connect perfectly. I had just bought a new encyclopedia on Compact Disc for my computer. As I was leisurely scanning through its contents, I "accidentally" made a most exciting discovery for my research on activating the genius. My mind was actually a million miles away from any thought of the book, but there was what I had been seeking, boldly leaping from the computer screen and into my awareness. What I found was not listed under "genius," it was in the section called "mythology" -- a place I would never have considered to look for genius stuff. But because I was enthusiastic about my writing, had kept a focus on my goal, and was flexible enough to recognize the opportunity before me, I experienced a fantastic discovery. In a nutshell, this is what it said:

In Roman mythology a Genius was a guardian spirit that protected an individual throughout his or her life. Every living person was endowed with a specific genius to whom yearly offerings were made, generally on the person's birthday. In addition to the individual's genius there were genii who protected tribes, towns, places, and the Roman State. A particularly important genius was the Genius Populi Romani, guardian of Rome. The accomplishments of an individual were often attributed to his or her genius.[1]

Although this Roman myth about geniuses being guardian spirits might not be all that believable today, it does, as does most mythology, draw upon some deeper inherent

---

[1] The New Grolier Multimedia Encyclopedia

truths. We all possess an inner guidance, one that is greater than the conscious mind. When you learn to tap into this power, you are, in all reality, awakening your genius. You will know it when it happens, and others will consider you a genius as well. This part of your mind is beyond what is conscious to you and is aware of even the minutest details of your life. There is only one thing stopping you from accessing this genius part of the mind; you were never taught how to access and use it.

Think of a computer for a moment. Even with all of its incredible capabilities, if you remove all the programs it is instantly rendered useless. The full potential is still there, inside the computer, but there is no software to make it work. Is this not how we are all born? We are equipped with the hardware, but with very little knowledge of the software. Our parents, family and friends built most of the programs. These programs may or may not be working in their lives, but if they're not, how on earth can you expect them to work for you?

As you read these secrets you will discover that it doesn't matter whether your parents are scholars, factory workers or alcoholics, the principles found here will help you to understand the mind and its awesome, never-ending ability to work for you. You may find yourself setting goals and achieving them, without ever knowing you have put forth the effort. Whether you want to become an academic wizard, build a perfect memory and recall, simply learn the processes of time management, or become President or Prime

Minister, the basics are all here. Enjoy, and allow yourself to experience your mind to the Ph.D. level. You can only attain the "Ph.D. of the Mind" by applying the techniques for yourself.

"The world belongs to the energetic."

Ralph Waldo Emerson

SECRET #3 ENERGIZING YOUR GENIUS

N -- STANDS FOR NON-STOP ENERGY

Once there was a little boy who hated school. He was held back in second grade and his parents were told that he had learning disabilities. Not that his parents were much help at that time; his father was struggling with alcoholism and his mother was doing her best to raise nine children, essentially on her own. The boy struggled each year and each year he fell further and further behind. He became the class clown and the teachers knew him as a troublemaker. People around him began affirming his negative attitude. They said he would never amount to anything. They said he was destined to end up an alcoholic. They said he was no good.

Something happened that changed this boy's life. As his father made the journey out of alcoholism, he began to learn about new ways of thinking that could, in turn, create new ways of living. He began recognizing how his thinking continued to get him into the same kind of trouble time after time. As he learned, he passed his newfound knowledge along to his children. Now this young man began taking to heart all that his father was teaching him. He realized that the one constant in his life was himself; the teachers, schools and situations would change, but he was the common denominator. He realized that if he changed, then everything around him would have to change too! He began to set goals and take action to achieve them. In a short period of time he made the honor-roll. His leadership abilities began to shine through. He became involved in sports and eventually achieved the status of three-sport captain and earned a college scholarship. This "learning disabled" troublemaker is today the author of an award-winning book called **Awaken the Genius**.

I will often tell people how fortunate I was to have been born the child of an alcoholic. Without my father's "problem," I may never have discovered at that young age that genius is not what some lucky someone is born into, but rather, genius is recognizing my own unique talents and skills and using them! I have developed a non-stop energy that is always moving me in the direction of my goals.

Let's see if you can guess of whom I am speaking by the descriptions given:

1. This child was born with an unusually large head. His mother did not agree with those who said the child was abnormal. He was sent to school, but was thought by the teacher to be mentally ill. The mother withdrew the child from school and taught him herself. This child's mother had no concept of failure and she passed this attitude along to her son. This young man had developed such non-stop energy, that he went so far as to attempt creating a light bulb out of peanut butter! People must have rolled their eyeballs and exclaimed, 'What a waste of time!" True, these efforts failed miserably, but he was not really trying to invent a light bulb with peanut butter; he was freeing his creative mind to formulate a solution. He may not have understood the "method behind his madness," but psychologists now understand that he was balancing the

power in his mind and giving energy to his true goal.[2]

2. This boy could not talk until age four. He did not learn to read until he was nine. His teacher called him unsociable and a dreamer. He failed entrance exams to college, but finally passed after an additional year of preparation. During the two years after graduation he obtained, and lost, three teaching positions. He became a patent clerk. To the people who knew him, he was a dreamer. He told people that he made his greatest discovery by imagining himself sitting on the tip of a light beam and being projected into space.[3]

3. When he was twelve years old he could not read, and remained deficient in reading all his life. However, he could memorize entire lectures, which was how he got through school. He became a famous general during World War II.[4]

By these examples, I hope that you can now recognize that the children going off to school each day are by no means finished products. They are in a perpetual state of change. In their

---

[2] Thomas Edison is known the world over as the inventor of the light bulb and the phonograph.

[3] Albert Einstein is a world-renowned physicist, best known for his theory of relativity.

[4] George Patton is one of the most well known war strategists of the twentieth century.

own unique way, they are learning, growing, and absorbing from the world around them. They are bursting with a genius potential that we can all help to bring forth.

I have heard so many people say, if only I had this skill or that knowledge, I might also experience success. I agree life would certainly be much easier if simply obtaining some ability or gaining new knowledge would guarantee success. Unfortunately, this isn't necessarily true.

Geniuses know better than to measure achievement by an end result. The true genius has learned to virtually embrace success through a series of day-to-day actions. These are actions that can be tested and repeated and that bring about a feeling of progress. This feeling invigorates and energizes. *Non-stop energy* is its by-product.

Geniuses recognize that their time is of great value, they can't afford the luxury of wasting a single minute. As you actively awaken your genius, you can enjoy the on-going enlightening (lightening of your mental load) that comes naturally when you are making a difference.

"The march of invention has clothed mankind with powers of which a century ago the boldest imagination could not have dreamt."

Henry George

"Great discoveries and improvements invariably involve the cooperation of many minds. I may be given credit for having blazed the trail but when I look at the subsequent developments I feel the credit is due to others rather than to myself."

Alexander Graham Bell

SECRET #4
INVENT YOUR GENIUS

I -- STANDS FOR IMAGINATION, CREATIVITY & INVENTIVENESS

Once upon a time there was a young man who had a dream for the world. He often fantasized about a planet at peace, with a clean environment and good health for all. This young man truly believed this world would be possible in his lifetime and set his sights to its creation. His dream had inspired his incredibly inventive mind.

Now there were many people with ideas very different from this young man's vision. Their plans involved greed and self-centeredness and so they challenged every one of his ideas and concepts. In jealousy and fear, they simply could not, or would not, believe that his mind could be that much more inventive and creative than their own. So one day he agreed to meet their challenge head on. He gave them the detailed directions for building a new kind of motor, one that would be much more efficient than those currently in production. They built the motor to his exact specifications. He then asked them to run the motor for an exact period of time while he went to another room and ran the motor in his imagination.

When he emerged from the room, he held a crumpled piece of paper in his hand with figures scribbled upon it. He directed the researchers to take the motor apart and to measure the exact wear upon the inner parts. To their astonishment, Mr. Nikola Tesla had scribbled the exact same measurements of wear as the researchers found with their precision instruments and he had done it all with his inventive mind.

Most of the true geniuses, such as Nikola Tesla, had little concern for fame or riches. These are simply the natural by-products of doing what one loves to do. If you don't know who Mr. Tesla was, don't feel alone. Very few people are familiar with Tesla's inventions. Yet his discoveries have had an incredible impact on the development of society as we know it today. Tesla is best known as the person responsible for creating alternating current (AC), which he patented and later sold to George Westinghouse. He had a vision of the world where all people could share in free energy. Sadly, many of Tesla's inventions never made it because there was no profit in free energy. While he was alive he never obtained the fame or wealth that he rightly deserved. Only now is he beginning to receive the recognition he merited for his many great inventions.

The Tesla Coil is still in use today and many of his other inventions, like Leonardo da Vinci's, will take years, perhaps even millennia, to come to fruition. How many other geniuses never received the recognition they rightly merited? We can only speculate. But over four billion geniuses are now equipped to take the path of discovery. When each "genius in training" passes into the great undiscovered country, each will leave behind a legacy in his or her own way.

So like the best known genius of our time, Albert Einstein, who believed life was exciting and sleep was a waste, we could collectively start living our dreams; building a world of common everyday geniuses working together to leave a legacy of growth and development. Discovery of the human potential, the truly undiscovered country, is the three-pound universe that exists in each of our heads.

Have you ever sat in a classroom listening to a lecturer and about halfway through noticed yourself growing so exhausted that you just had to let your mouth stretch into a yawn. Perhaps your head began to feel like a lead weight, as if your chin was magnetically drawn to your chest. It is the overload placed on the left hemisphere of the brain that causes this type of sleepiness. The left brain can be likened to a computer filing system--with a few vast differences. Human intelligence is far superior to even the most sophisticated computer system for one profound reason. The brain not only stores and processes information, it also records each bit of information with emotion. In this very real way your brain stores information holographically.

Think for a moment about "apple pie."

Perhaps you can see the apple pie in your mind or imagination. Maybe you are able to recall the sweet, apple-cinnamon scent of a pie just coming out of a hot oven. Were you, perchance, like one seminar participant who stood before the group and described how she could see her grandmother's broad smile, and her face, a multitude of crinkles that reflected many years of joy, worry, laughter and sorrow. She told us about Grandma's frail little arms that were tucked into huge oven mitts and of the love she felt as she watched Grandmother slowly work her way to the dinner table with her beautifully crafted creation. The family would ooh and aah appreciatively as they inhaled the rich aroma and allowed Grandma's steaming apple pie to melt in their mouths. This young woman was remembering hot apple pie holographically. All the senses of sight, smell, taste, touch, and sound are involved.

All of this holographic processing takes energy--mental energy. It would be logical then that a key ingredient to genius would be to find a way to think holographically, but without expending so much mental energy. A genius understands the power within the process by which the five senses bring information into the brain. By using that power, the learning experience becomes a natural flow so that, just like turning a doorknob, it requires little or no thought.

I feel fortunate to have met and become friends with a true genius and a master of holographic thinking. This gentleman is extremely gifted in the field of computers and in the art of invention. When I first met Jerry, I considered him rather eccentric. His home, inside and out, was stacked with junk. I asked him how he could find anything in such a mess; let alone come up with inventions from an absolute scrap heap. (Jerry builds all of his prototypes from scraps and old parts.) He related an extraordinary story.

When Jerry was a small child, he would fall into deep, peaceful sleep and dream of all that he wanted to build. This in itself was not uncommon. Most young boys at one time or another will dream of fame and riches as a renowned inventor. Unlike other boys, however, Jerry never grew out of it. With each passing year his dreams grew more vivid. This slumber world became real to him as he developed a keen memory that held every detail intact. To this day Jerry uses his dream world to uncover solutions to his problems or those of his clients. (He is also a computer consultant.) He dreams about these solutions holographically.

While most people discredit their nighttime counsel as "just a dream," Jerry has trained his mind to create his full presence in the experience. In his mind, he is there, seeing through his eyes, hearing through his ears and sensing and feeling with his body. What's most amazing is that upon awakening Jerry can recall every detail of just how he is to build the device of which he dreamed. Jerry knows that if he gets to a point where stress or frustration is building up, he can simply take a brief nap of ten to fifteen minutes. Invariably the solution to his stress will come to him upon awakening.

I believe that everyone is imbued with some special talent or skill (genius). Sometimes the talent is obvious, such as the athlete or musician. Others are much more obscure--the born organizer, troubleshooter or mediator. Perhaps some just require more polish than others do. Even people like Jerry, who clearly demonstrates a special gift, must choose to make it shine. Have you ever known an over-achieving athlete who went from being a "98-pound weakling" to captain of the football team? It has been said that geniuses aren't born, they are made. We can't all be like Jerry (nor would we want to be), but we can learn from his methods to attain a sense of genius in our own right.

"It is difficult to say what is impossible, for the dream of yesterday is the hope of today and the reality of tomorrow."

--Robert H. Goddard

"The improvement of our way of life is more important than the spreading of it. If we make it satisfactory enough, it will spread automatically. If we do not, no strength of arms can permanently oppose it."

--Charles A. Lindbergh

"The only limit to our realization of tomorrow will be our doubts of today. Let us move forward with strong and active faith."

--Franklin Delano Roosevelt

SECRET #5
TRUST YOUR GENIUS

U-- STANDS FOR UNENDING DRIVE TO SUCCEED

Thomas Edison, known the world over as the inventor of the light bulb, was once asked how he managed to keep himself motivated while working on a project. Edison recalled that when inventing the light bulb, he had experienced 999 failures prior to his discovery. His response was a simple but profound one. "I didn't fail 999 times at creating the light bulb," he replied; "I found 999 ways in which it just won't work."

What did Edison have that seemingly eludes most people? His ability to restructure his thinking so that no matter what happened, it was a success. What others would perceive as failure was, to him, feedback. It is this attitude that creates a genius.

Sound a little too simple to you? It can't possibly be that easy to become a genius, you might say. Perhaps you thought that to be a genius you must first pop the top off the IQ charts.

The kind of genius I'm talking about is, like Edison, popping the top off the scale of the "I do" quotient. You might know the type of people who get more done with fewer resources. These are the gifted ones who make things happen! Whether or not you consider yourself a genius, you can count on your brain never to make a liar out of you. If you enter into an activity with success in mind, your genius will continue to work out the details, and seek out all necessary resources, until you are successful.

It has been said that 5% of the people get 95% of the work done. Not surprisingly, 5% of the population also holds about 95% of the wealth in the world!

You are what you think about all day long.

Your brain works like a computer in several ways. A computer operates on much more than just a control box, keyboard and a monitor. Yet these are the parts of which you are visibly aware. There are innumerable unseen internal parts that allow incredible mathematical functions to take place.

The key ingredient for any computer to function is its operating system. In computer jargon, this is usually a program called Data Operating System (DOS). Without this program your computer will not run. Your brain also has a DOS program and it consists of your beliefs and values.

Let's start with belief systems. One of my favorite statements is, ***"The law of mind is the law of belief."*** What does this mean? Simply that whether you believe you are smart, or believe that everyone else is more intelligent than you are, you are right! The mind will support you with the appropriate behaviors that will uphold your belief. This is why people who believe themselves to be unintelligent will sabotage their success in some way. If they do well on a test, they might say, "It was just luck." Then, on the very next test, they may fail miserably to bring their percentage back into a comfort zone.

A genius is not afraid to stretch the comfort zone, to go beyond perceived limits, and is smart enough to know that there is no failure, there is only feedback. This attitude is the formula for an unending drive to succeed.

So what about values? Values work beyond the conscious level and motivate us either to take action or retreat. Some people believe that values are learned through life's experiences and that once learned they are almost impossible to change. But geniuses are capable of self-analysis. They will ask, "Is there a better way for me to act, to think, to feel, to be?" These are the people who take charge, are flexible and make changes whenever necessary. They learn early in life to cope with that over which they have no choice. A true genius manages and handles frustration.

How do you start the process of tapping into your unending drive to succeed? You can start by identifying it. Gain an understanding of who you really are. Right this very moment, at work within you, there is an internal genius with an absolute blueprint for success. It is somehow monitoring the seventy-five trillion cells of your body and replacing those cells at the rate of fifty million or more per second. It remembers to beat your heart 86,000 times per day. It remembers to breathe 21,000 times each day. Can you imagine what would happen if you had to consciously remember to breathe, or beat your heart, or build new cells? Someone would need to follow you with a wheelbarrow to pick up your arms and legs because you might forget to build the needed cells at the right time. Just notice how your eyes are scanning across this page and, believe it or not, your super-conscious mind has already absorbed every word printed here. It is all happening automatically and with incomprehensible precision and accuracy. Now that's sheer genius, and it's right there, naturally, within you!

*"The universe is full of magical things
patiently waiting for our wits to grow sharper."*

Eden Phillpotts

SECRET #6
GENIUS IS ALL ATTITUDE

S -- STANDS FOR SPONTANEOUS INTUITIVE BREAKTHROUGHS

It was one of those spring storms that came out of nowhere. The beach was chaos as tourists and local vendors scattered in every direction trying to find shelter from the storm. Monstrous waves crashed against the shoreline. They ripped claw-like into the sand, digging deep rifts where children had been building sand castles only minutes earlier. Mother Nature had proved her supremacy once again.

Just as quickly as the storm had appeared, it now vanished into a distant gray rumble. The beach was cleared of the human clutter, but a new kind of chaos took its place; it was breathtaking as the sunlight danced across a sparkling array of stranded starfish. There were thousands of them scattered everywhere. As the children returned to the beach, some of the boys began to throw the starfish back into the now calm sea. It gave them a sense of pride to know they were helping the marooned little creatures.

Just then an elderly man approached. He walked with an odd swinging gait as he slowly dragged a partially lame foot across the sand. The old man had a forbidding air about him and most children moved in another direction whenever he came around. He liked it that way.

The old man stopped his halting gait and watched the boys for a moment. "Stop that," he called, "Can't you see that what you're doing isn't going to make any difference ...none at all!? This beach goes on for hundreds of miles! It's loaded with stranded starfish just like these. What you're doing won't matter a bit, not one bit! "

The boys stood as if frozen and eyed the wintry old man, unsure of how to respond to his demands. The youngest of the boys gazed thoughtfully at the starfish closest to his feet. He quietly picked up the starfish and cast it out into the ocean. He turned to the elder and calmly stated, "It mattered to that one."

THE HUNDREDTH MONKEY

The Japanese monkey Macaca Fuscata has been observed in the wild for a period of over 40 years. In 1952, on the island of Koshima, scientists were providing monkeys with sweet potatoes dropped in the sand. The monkeys liked the taste of the raw sweet potatoes, but they found the dirt quite unpleasant. An 18-month-old female named Imo had a spontaneous intuitive breakthrough. She found she could solve the problem by washing the potatoes in a nearby stream. She taught this trick to her mother. Her playmates also learned this new way and they taught their mothers too. Various monkeys during the course of the scientific experiment gradually picked up this cultural innovation.

Between 1952 and 1958, all the young monkeys learned to wash the sandy sweet potatoes to make them more palatable. Only the adults who imitated their children learned this social improvement. The other adults kept eating the dirty sweet potatoes. Then something startling took place. In the autumn of 1958, a certain number of Koshima monkeys were washing sweet potatoes. The exact number is not known. Let us suppose that when the sun rose one morning there were 99 monkeys on Koshima Island who had learned to wash their sweet potatoes. Let's further suppose that later that morning the hundredth monkey learned to wash potatoes. Then it happened! By that evening almost everyone in the tribe was washing sweet potatoes before eating them. The added energy of this hundredth monkey somehow created a spontaneous ideological breakthrough! What was most surprising to these scientists was that the habit of washing sweet potatoes then spontaneously jumped over the sea. Colonies of monkeys on other islands as well as the mainland troop of monkeys at Takasakiyama began washing their sweet potatoes!

Thus, it would seem that when a certain critical number achieves genius awareness, this new awareness might be communicated from mind to mind. Although the exact number may vary, the Hundredth Monkey Phenomenon means that when only a limited number of people are exposed to an innovation, it remains the property of these people. But there is a specific point at which, if only one more person tunes in to a new awareness, it becomes available to the whole of humanity.

Experimental psychologists later proved the Hundredth Monkey Phenomenon in rat water maze tests conducted over a period of 35 years, first in America, then in Scotland and finally in Australia. The results showed that the rats became better and better in escaping from the maze as time went on and that this increased ability to learn was then transmitted geographically. The rats in Scotland learned quicker than the original subjects in America. Those in Australia learned fastest of all. This increased ability to learn affected all rats of the same breed whether or not they descended from trained parents. They demonstrated this transmission of acquired understanding beyond the "usual" concepts of learning. Today's geniuses realize that we are all in this together.

What does all this Hundredth Monkey Phenomenon mean to you as an awakening genius? Perhaps that you are not only awakening yourself but also the inner genius of those around you! In today's modern world, we are bombarded with thousands of times more information than the people who lived at the turn of the century. Yet the onslaught of information seems to have little or no effect on us; or so we think. The reality is that our internal genius, that part of our mind that is other-than-conscious, has been protecting us, gently teaching us how to manage such massive amounts of information.

Many of our world's greatest inventions and discoveries were by people who were considered to have average or lesser intelligence. Remember that Albert Einstein failed his first college entrance exam! Yet just like the laboratory rats that collectively made getting through the maze easier and easier, these geniuses went against the odds; they created the hundredth monkey effect, and helped humanity out of the maze.

Are you now living within the confines of the maze? Do you feel trapped by what others have told you? Does someone or something else do your thinking for you? It's never too late to move out of the maze; to wake up and use that untapped 95% of your brain. With your creativity, you could be the "one" who sparks the rest of humanity.

If you were a Vulcan, like Mr. Spock of Star Trek fame, you would probably have an incredibly active left brain. Like Spock, the left brain seeks logic; it believes in control and precision. The left brain is sequential and, therefore, everything in this area must make sense. Whether you are verbally communicating with another person, working out mathematical equations, balancing your checkbook or solving a word game, you are using the left brain. Today's school systems operate primarily with left brain processing through memorization. That is why some students find school to be a big YAWN. These kids are usually the "Right Brainers." (We'll discuss them next.)

Unfortunately, there is one small glitch with the overactive left brain's logical and linear way of thinking. It assumes that all information is 100% accurate just as it stands. No problem, unless you were trained with improper or inappropriate beliefs and values. If this is the case, the logical thinking of the left brain can end up controlling you with negative self-fulfilling prophecies. As an example, a student firmly believes that she is no good at algebra and then proves herself right by consistently failing examinations in math class. It is certainly no coincidence that most addictions or problem behaviors stem from left brain functions. The person with an over-active left brain locks out the creativity that could otherwise present an optional behavior or alternative method for success.

The Left-Brain is not concerned with what is true; it is only affected by what is truth for you. Your truth is based on the evidence you have gathered throughout your life experience, whether real or imagined. This information is your judge and jury. It controls and plans your future because the left brain also monitors time.

Now don't get me wrong, the left brain functions are a necessary part of day-to-day thinking. My hope is that by now you are enlightened to the possibility that maybe, just maybe, the way your left brain was trained has caused it to stand in the way of your success.

When I was a child I used to marvel at the mind of the inventor. How did these geniuses ever come up with their original ideas? Why hadn't anyone ever thought of it before? How did they know it would really work? Was their brain any different than mine? Their heads didn't look any bigger than mine or anyone else's. As I grew up and made my own discoveries, these questions never completely left my mind, and, to be honest, the answers were a long time in coming. I was curious, and it was this sense of wonder that attracted me to the fields of psychology and counseling. I have since drawn many of my own conclusions and this is one of which I am certain: Those people possessing right-brain dominant features have a better opportunity for making changes and becoming balanced in their thinking.

The right brain is responsible for our ability to be creative; it is the ability to dream. The musical and artistic skills are products of the right brain. Some consider these features to be more feminine in nature, although men and women can be equally creative and artistic. The right brain is a wonderful, free-spirited place to live. It is the place of dreams and visions, fantasies and fairy tales, freedom, imagination, romance and make-believe. It is a place that knows no boundaries or limitations

Sound wonderful? It is. But for some, it can be a dangerous place too. When people allow themselves to become too right-brain dominant in this left-brain world, they are setting themselves up for trouble. How long does one last in our present society with the inability to balance a checkbook, or to perform simple mathematics, or stay focused on the basic laws of English?

A genius realizes that true power is in neither the left nor the right brain functions but in the ability to fluctuate between them according to what is needed at the time. When the left brain is equipped to work in conjunction with the right brain, harmony will occur. It is in this state of harmony that optimism and hope can flourish, it is where spontaneous intuitive breakthroughs are free flowing. Einstein once said that the mind works like a parachute: it works best when open! If the left brain is closed to new ideas, the powerful flow of the mind will cease. The average Joe sees life as a series of problems, while a genius sees life as a series of discoveries and solutions.

The True Power of Your Mind Does Not Reside In Knowledge.

I am a great admirer of Albert Einstein. It is obvious that Einstein knew how to use his brain to get results. I even have a giant-sized poster of young Einstein hanging in my office. I bought it not so much for his picture, but because of a simple yet profound quotation printed along the side of his face. He tells us, "Imagination is more important than knowledge." I believe it was this simple wisdom that led Einstein to his greatest discoveries. If you really want to open up to greater possibilities, you must open up your creative right brain functions to work in harmony with your logical mind. Remember how Edison once tried to create a light bulb from peanut butter? This was his way of gaining access to his highly imaginative and inventive right brain. He was creating the space in his mind for a spontaneous intuitive breakthrough!

As I researched the many geniuses of our time and of long ago, I was amazed to find that a good number of the great inventors of the past were also artists. Leonardo da Vinci, one of the greatest artists of all time, was also an extraordinary inventor. Leonardo had a curious mind, and he often directed his artistic talent toward scientific endeavors. He used his drawing skills to convey his scientific conceptions. Most of his inventions, however, were much too advanced for his generation. His drawings revealed what he conceived for the future: flying machines, parachutes, helicopters, underwater diving suits, a protective tank for battle and methods of automation, to name just a few. The tools and known resources of the period could not come close to producing that which his imagination could so clearly create. Most of Leonardo's inventions were unknown until the 20th Century, when several of his notebooks were found. Interestingly, these notes were all written in a bizarre right-to-left script that could only be read with a mirror. We can only speculate as to his purpose in writing the notes in such a peculiar manner. Yet clearly these are the writings of an incredibly creative mind.

***

ARE YOU A GENIUS?

Now that you have reached the end of this text, you might be thinking to yourself, am I a genius?

My answer is a most emphatic YES! You have the six secrets. You have demonstrated every one of these six attributes at some time in your life. You know that you were born with **Secret #1**, the *genuine positive attitude*, built right in. You could still have problems popping the top off the IQ charts. But now you know that IQ is not an accurate test of genius. Now you are your own judge. For you, the real test will be in putting together a life of fulfilled dreams.

I have heard it said that people don't plan to fail, they fail to plan! If you have not yet put together a game plan for your life, now is the time. Go ahead, make your goals real and tangible by putting them down on paper. Dare to truly dream your dreams. Remember what the good book says, "Faith without works is dead." This is precisely what Edison meant when he said genius is 1% inspiration and 99% perspiration. It is not always the swiftest person who wins the race. Rather, it is the individual with **Secret #2**, *enthusiasm, focus* *and flexibility*, who goes out and overcomes all obstacles to make it happen.

THE GENIUS MIND-SET

Geniuses know exactly where they are going; they know what they want to achieve. Perhaps they are not yet aware of how, specifically, they will get there, but they know the direction in which they are headed. Because of this attitude, they have **Secret #3**, *non-stop energy*.

A genius never gives up. He or she has the ability to improvise. A genius learns early in life that there are no victims. They have chosen their place in the great scope of life and if they don't like where they are, then it is up to them to change. Geniuses understand that they are in full control of one universe. It weighs about three pounds and exists inside their own head. Geniuses also know that there is a source and power far greater than their little human form that controls and shapes the destiny of the human condition. It resides in their other-than-conscious mind.

If given the opportunity, would you change any portion of your past? If you said "yes" to changing even one small segment of your past, then you have given a direct suggestion to your other-than-conscious mind to go back through your memory banks and clean up old behaviors or perhaps clear away a limited belief. You have just engaged **Secret #4**, *imagination, creativity and inventiveness*. A genius knows that the greatest control comes from taking command of one's own mind and that the control is in letting go. I know that this seems like a contradiction in terms, but it is completely true.

What would happen if you could look at a problem with the eyes of wonder? And you said to yourself, I wonder how great things will be when I solve this problem and get on with my life? This simple question will instill **Secret #5**, the *unending drive to succeed*. You will easily proceed to solve the problem with the attitude that the solution is at hand, even if you have no idea what it is! The real "brains" in this world know that our minds store solutions with problems and problems with solutions.

As a modern-day genius, your task is to focus on solutions and simply use problems as stepping stones to even greater success. Then you will have a natural and unlimited supply of **Secret #6**, *spontaneous intuitive breakthroughs*.

Now that you are aware of the six secrets of G.E.N.I.U.S., you have naturally and effortlessly sparked your genius potential. Even if you don't believe it, your mind has been affected by what you have read in these pages. The secrets have been activated!

Are you willing to believe in a world of geniuses where peace and the pursuit of collective happiness are the founding principles? We are on a journey. It will not end with us, just as it did not begin with us. What part of your genius will you leave behind for future generations to use?

It is my hope and prayer that you will choose to be a herald of the new generation; that with your awakened genius you will strive to surpass those misguided individuals who are currently leaving a legacy of pollution and social injustice in the pursuit of their own desires.

True geniuses work to benefit all of humankind, knowing that as they help those around them, they are naturally helping themselves. I commend you for the commitment you have made to awaken your full potential, to building a planet of harmony, and to developing and living your dreams.

"See you geniuses in the future!"

Positive Changes Hypnosis Centers ®
YOUR FRANCHISE OPPORTUNITY

Are you looking for a rewarding, people-helping profession that also fulfills your entrepreneurial and financial dreams? Positive Changes is waiting for you!

Positive Changes Hypnosis Centers ® is a unique, all-inclusive and gratifying business opportunity that is taking the self-help industry by storm! We are actively seeking people who believe in the power and success of Positive Changes' programs to join our growing network of franchise locations. Together we can offer affordable assistance to people, just like you, who are looking to make lasting lifestyle improvements.

PCH is meeting a demand as North America's first and only franchised network of hypnosis professionals. Our success is based on our one-of-a-kind programs, products and testimonials from those clients whom we have helped along the way. By offering more than 140 various pre-recorded hypnosis programs, we can provide client services for virtually any problem.

We provide all of our franchise owners with thorough training in the operation of their center, hypnosis training and a complete franchise package that will support you in opening your center and running it day-to-day. To get started, all you need is the desire to succeed and we will provide you with the rest!

Our amazing business formula is uniquely Positive Changes and is a result of years of research and operational testing. As an owner, you will be provided with a proven step-by-step program used in all PCH centers across the U.S. and Canada. You will be supplied with everything you need to operate your center.

As you are well aware, consumers in the self-improvement industry are extremely focused on results. PCH has set our services apart from the

rest of the self-improvement pack, offering consumers something new, long lasting and effective.

Recognized by the American Medical Association, hypnosis is an effective method of behavior modification that is non-therapeutic, 100% safe and has no side effects. Over the years, we have gathered moving testimonials and photos from weight-loss, smoking and other clients who have had great success with our services. We will supply you with these testimonials, a suggested advertising schedule, product catalogs, marketing materials, a Positive Changes Today? newsletter, state of the art website,

direct mail campaigns and much, much more. Testimonials are the driving force behind getting new clients through your door. We'll even show you how to effectively gather testimonials from your own clients.

Because of the success and presence of PCH and its franchisees, the market for consumer hypnosis services is growing rapidly. A franchise provides you with many advantages like extensive training, access to recognized logos and brand names, strong marketing materials and advertising power.

Remember, there is NO hypnosis experience required. We are looking for caring, entrepreneurial individuals that believe in the success of Positive Changes. Actually, most of our current franchisees had no experience or background in hypnosis, counseling or medicine. They simply recognized PCH as a great way to help others attain health and happiness, be their own boss and make success happen!

PCH will train you, provide you with assistance in finding the perfect location for your center, recruit and train your staff, provide tools, forms and checklists you need for daily operations and much more! We will show you how to form partnerships with local doctors to gain referrals and how to retain current clients, while growing your list of new clients. You will receive everything you need to run a successful center.

As the ONLY source of PCH products and hypnosis services, Positive Changes Hypnosis and its franchisees have no direct competition. The fact that our sales have grown 45% annually over the last two years is indicative of the demand for our services.

What are you waiting for? PCH is ready for you! To receive a franchise information package and application, please call 843-853-4781 or e-mail your mailing address to:

franchiseinfo@ihypnosis.net

PCH Franchise Headquarters
474 Wando Park Blvd., Suite 200
Mt. Pleasant, SC 29464
1-800-771-7866
www.positivechanges.com

Personalize Your Success with
Hypnosis to Go!

Naturally Thin

Learn to eat and think like a naturally thin person, conquer your cravings, increase your self-confidence, and plan for a lifetime of weight loss success! Here are just a few of the titles available!

* Develop the Characteristics of Naturally Thin People
* End Roller Coaster Weight Loss
* Evaporate Cravings and Hunger Pains
* Extinguish Sugar and Chocolate Addiction
* Convert Your Body into a Fat-Burning Machine
* Eliminate Overweight Behaviors and Patterns

Smoking Cancellation

Kick your smoking habit for good using the proven strategies in this series. Conquer your cravings and extinguish the stress and frustration associated with quitting smoking. Break the chains that have bound you to cigarettes and be tobacco free forever!

* Avoiding the Usual Quitting Traps
* Eliminate the Anchors That Create the Habit
* Relaxation and the Non-Smoker
* Tobacco-Free at Work
* Conquer Cravings and Be Tobacco-Free
* Extinguish Stress and Frustration
* Going with the Flow Tobacco-Free
* Tobacco-Free By the Numbers
* Planning a Lifetime Tobacco-Free

Mind Mastery

Choose the hypnosis processes that best suit your needs for creating limitless personal change and success in your life. Ask about our discount when you purchase all seven!

* Activate Your Personal Success
* Put a Dead Halt to Self-Sabotage
* Keys that Create Success
* Trying New Things
* Stimulate Optimistic Thinking
* Building Motivation and Drive
* Release Fear & Doubt

Pain Free with Hypnosis

Overcome the hold pain has on your life with these hypnotic processes that teach you to manage pain using the most powerful pharmacy on Earth— your subconscious mind!

Accelerated Learning

Overcome learning challenges with this amazing series! Increase your reading speed, improve your memory, get organized and earn better grades with our complete learning system.

Sales Mastery

Discover the powerful selling methods of sales masters! Build your self-confidence, master your time, and learn to overcome objections, with this amazing series.

Sports Excellence

Discover how hypnosis can enhance your enjoyment of the game you love! Use this tape series to mentally rehearse your success and instill the right mind-set before you play. Learn simple techniques for improving poise and concentration.

Self-Mastery through Self-Hypnosis

Enjoy the luxury of self-hypnosis any time you desire once you've mastered the art of self-hypnosis. This audio set makes learning to hypnotize yourself easy and fun! You can use the techniques to improve your life in 1,001 different ways!

Other Books Available at www.HypnosisToGo.com

Awaken the Genius
"Mind Technology For The 21st Century"

Psycho-Linguistics
"The Language of the Mind"

Find out more about advanced bio-feed-in equipment at
www.HypnosisToGo.com

Positive Changes Hypnosis® has quickly become the global authority in the field of hypnosis. If it is time for you to make a change, go to www.PositiveChanges.com and find a center near you.

"Where Results Happen"

If you would like a complete catalog please go to www.HypnosisToGo.com and sign up on line.